Addicts & Infidels

Cheri Lovedog

ISBN: 1475034512
ISBN-13: 9781475034516

*To my mom Marilyn, my brother
Mike, and my sister Celeste,
for your undying and unconditional
love, support, and faith in me.
All of which I'd lost in myself too
many times to count. I wouldn't
be here, literally, without you.
Seriously. You have no idea.*

*To Sylvia Brown & Robert...
all gratitude and love.*

*Also, to every girl who ever broke my
heart, um... thanks for the inspiration?
Yes, absolutely, thank you.*

*And for the one who won't, I look
forward to meeting you.*

FOREWORD

I divide my life into two very distinct and unique phases: Pre Prozac, and Post Prozac.

Pre Prozac, I had some serious anger issues.

Here are some highlights:

My roommate had to keep me from beating a drunk guy to death with my baseball bat who was trying to break into my bedroom window at 3:30 am.

I would stomp around Hollywood in the middle of the night begging for confrontation. Any excuse to fuck someone up. Anybody. It didn't matter if I won or lost, I just needed the fight.

I was also quite fond of kicking and punching things. I kicked a water cooler so hard I ended up in the emergency room. I had injured my foot so badly, I spent some time on crutches, then on a cane. Needless to say, I only kicked a water cooler once.

I have no idea how many holes I have punched and kicked into walls, door, mirrors, etc., but I do have mad skills with a putty knife and spackle.

At my finest, I was strung out on valium, weighed 91 lbs, and was squatting in a vacant apartment my friends had moved out of.

I do not do those things anymore, or live like that anymore. Not since a week of the most out of control vertigo and panic attacks I had ever experienced led me to the emergency room.

The doctor who examined me gave me a prescription for Antivert, and recommended I see a psychiatrist. Immediately. He said the physical symptoms were, in fact, manifestations of psychological issues. If I didn't address them, it would continue for the rest of my life. Who knew?

So, I went to the shrink, and was given my diagnosis: PTSD, Borderline Agoraphobia, and blah, blah, blah. The recommended treatment was intense therapy and medications.

I was not thrilled with the idea of digging up and sharing my personal hell, which most people call a childhood, with a complete stranger. I had no problem writing about it all, but saying it out loud is quite another story.

And I initially resisted the medications out of fear. I was afraid it would hinder or eliminate my desire to write. Writing was *the only thing* I have *ever* been consistent at in my *entire* life. I mean, at least I knew who I was at that point: A fucking mess who identified as a writer. Hell, I'd even had some success at it. A play I wrote, entitled *Prey for Rock and Roll*, got produced in NYC.

I was in the process of rewriting the play into a screenplay when the annoying, yet life altering Panic Attack/Vertigo/Emergency Room Incident of 2002 occurred.

So if I couldn't write, what/who the fuck would I be? My shrink assured me that if I were a writer, a *real* writer, the medication would not get in the way. So I took the damn pills. Long story short, she was right. I finished writing the screenplay, the movie got made and went on to kill it at film festivals all around the world. I also wrote and produced a second feature film entitled *All American Gender Outlaw*.

I would love to say the Prozac has cured me in every way, and I am completely normal and well adjusted. Or that it eliminated my weird OCD trips. It didn't. I still purchase fruits in sets of three. The towels still must be hung on the rack with the folded side to the left, and the corner tag in the back. My laundry must be folded immediately out of the dryer, and in a very specific way. My salad cannot be on the same plate as my food. And so much more.

But I still write fearlessly, and I still take my little green and white pill daily. What I no longer do is self- sabotage or self-destruction. Oh, and my doors and walls are safe.

Zack Gaylord 1997

CHERI LOVEDOG

Pre Prozac

Post Prozac

Lyrics

ADDICTS AND INFIDELS

Pre Prozac

Self Indulgence as a Way of Life

I have so much to think about all the time.

So many problems

to work out.

So many insecurities

to cover up.

So many people

to avoid.

So much time

to waste.

So many decisions

to make.

So many debts

to worry about.

So much work

to put off.

So many ideas

to remember.

So many words

to look up in the dictionary.

So many cigarettes

to smoke.

Man,

I am

busy.

I have the Power of 10,000 Gods!

Here is something I do not understand:

You spend years of your life

with someone.

You in love with them,

and they in love with you.

They know all your secrets,

all the promises made,

and most of those broken.

They know all your dreams and desires,

and all your deviations.

They've made love to you,

and you to them,

thousands of times.

No thought too private that

it could not be shared.

And then,

when the love affair ends because

they want to go and find themselves,

and you let them

and get on with your life,

the phone rings six months later

and that familiar voice says,

"You're a vicious cunt

and

you ruined my life!"

Imagine

having the power

to do that.

My Mom

Why is it that I can work

two jobs

and still have trouble

paying the rent?

I'll tell you who can answer that question.

My Mom.

"Get a real job.

Bartending and working in a thrift store

are not real jobs.

You don't even have medical

and dental insurance.

Get a job in an office, or at a super market,

or at the Post Office."

"Mom, I don't want to."

"But your life would be so much easier

if you got a real job with medical and dental

insurance.

It would be a stable income and

stable hours.

All you have to do is:

a) Put aside your music until you are stable.

b) Take out your nose ring.

c) Cover your tattoos.

d) Let your hair grow.

e) Get a conservative wardrobe."

"Oh, is that all I have to do?

Stop being myself?"

"Be two people.

Do that during the day

and be yourself at night."

"I already am two people. At least.

I'll get confused. I can't do it.

I'd be selling myself out."

"You're too proud.

Right now, you need money.

Forget your pride."

"Mom… it's all I really have."

Girls will be Girls… Musicians will be Worse

Music

is everything.

How typical

to feel like that.

How typical to hear,

"Never marry a musician.

You'll always come second."

Really, it's third:

Music comes first.

Then me.

Then you.

Opposites Attract

You made me promise

that I would love you forever.

You've been gone a year.

You're not even here

to see

that I have kept my promise.

You, however, did not keep yours.

I wonder what will last longer?

My love for you?

Your hate for me?

Does it really matter?

Love or hate,

we both feel passion,

and we both know

we can never be together

again.

What makes that easier to live with?

Love or hate?

Obviously,

we don't see eye to eye

on that

either.

Thou Shall Not Kill

One of the hardest promises

I've ever had to keep

is that I would not commit murder.

Donald Paul Wolfe

married his second cousin

not too long ago,

and sells real estate

in Grandada Hills, California.

He is moving to Germany soon

and has taken up bowling,

I am told.

Twenty or so years ago

I was his stepdaughter.

He raped

and

molested

and

beat

and

degraded

and

humiliated

and

screamed at me

all the time.

He beat up my mom.

I don't think a day goes by

when I don't think of him.

He helped make me

the woman I am today.

Way to go, dad.

My Ex

I had a lover

for four years.

That's to say,

off and on

for four years.

Now

I have an EX lover,

for just about a year.

I think it had something to do with

the age difference.

I was eight years older,

not to mention

five broken hearts wiser.

So, my ex still calls now and then.

Calls me on the telephone.

Calls me names.

I don't mind,

because every time I see my ex

she looks constipated,

and never says a word to me

when we are face to face.

I think my ex still loves me.

Before, When I Wanted to Die

I lived in an apartment on Gardner Street.

I hated everyone.

I hated everything.

I hated myself.

I had a dog.

A big, beautiful red Doberman.

Her name was Sheena,

after the Ramones song.

I sat in that apartment

smoking three packs of cigarettes

a day.

Drinking endless pots of coffee.

Taking valium.

Listening to Joy Division.

I lost twenty pounds.

I looked dead.

I just did not care.

Then one day,

for reasons too numerous to mention,

I did care.

A LOT.

While I was getting better,

my dog got mange

and she had to be

put down.

Now I feel guilty

all the time.

I really did love that dog.

God,

I was such an asshole back then.

We Work Together

You never call

when I really want you to.

I can call you anytime

and it would be okay.

You are always glad I called.

You don't even know I fantasize about you.

Maybe I'll tell you about it

someday,

when it really doesn't matter anymore.

And we'll both laugh

and you'll say,

"Why didn't you say something?"

And I'll just shrug it off.

But I will think to myself,

"Why didn't you notice?"

Single as a Noun, Not a Verb

What is being single?

It sounds good

at clubs, at parties.

"I'm single."

But what does it really mean?

It means going out on dates with people

with the ambition of a kitchen table.

It means going out on dates with people

with the personality of a dial tone.

It means going out on dates with people

who can not form complete sentences.

It means going without sex,

because no sex

is better than bad sex.

It means finding someone you really like

BUT…

They drink too much.

Or take too many drugs.

Or they have a girlfriend.

Or all of the above.

It means deciding weather or not

to overlook those things.

It means masturbation.

I Have No Secrets

That's a lie.

I have a lot of secrets.

How come nobody gets close enough

to want to know them?

How come nobody gets close enough

to want to know me?

I am not bi-sexual.

I am not homo-sexual.

I am not hetro-sexual.

I am not anything,

unless I am with you.

Then I am sex.

I am mouth.

I am cunt.

I am sweat.

I am coming.

I am whatever

you want me to be.

I am whatever

you need me to be.

Sick Fuck Love

I sit here,

cigarette burning

in the ashtray,

thinking about blood.

Thinking about you.

Remembering writing

"I Love You"

on your stomach

in blood.

Your blood.

Blood from your cunt.

Blood from fucking you

(too?) hard.

Blood on my hands.

Blood in my mouth.

I really wanted to hurt you,

but I only made you bleed.

The Quandary

The worst thing

about not knowing

EXACTLY

what to do with my life,

is that I never know

just where to begin

doing anything.

So Easy to be Me

I didn't ask

to be who I am.

Then again, I never asked to be

anyone different.

I know people who wish they were

someone else,

specifically.

They say, "I wish I was her."

I wonder what the hell for?

A whole new set of problems, flaws and failures

to deal with?

I know mine so well

I would be afraid to trade them.

They work for me,

and I work for them.

When I get tired of one,

I move onto the next.

And the next.

And the next.

According to my Therapist

I'm holding on too tight.

I feel like I'm going to explode

all over the fucking place!

I am my own worst enemy.

I don't allow myself the luxury of trust.

I don't get close to people

because I'm afraid they'll leave.

I don't want a relationship

because I don't want to deal with it

ending.

And they always end,

I see to that.

As soon as I get in,

I start looking for a way out.

I start looking for monsters

where there are none.

And I find them.

Sometimes I want to scream,

"Whatever you do, don't love me!"

Because

I will pay such a high price

for allowing it.

By loving you,

I have armed you with enough weaponry

to successfully destroy me.

And that makes you

a potential enemy.

I am not a Morning Person

One of my biggest flaws

is that

in the morning,

until I've had a few cups of coffee

and smoked a few cigarettes,

I have no personality.

Fearless

I wish I could do

whatever I want,

with whom I want,

when I want,

where ever I want,

and feel safe

doing it.

I wish I didn't have to be

afraid

to walk outside at night.

I wish there was no such thing

as rape.

I wish there was no such thing

as violence.

There are hundreds of other things

that I wish were not.

But as I sit in my room

with my window closed and locked

on this beautiful Hollywood summer night,

these things come to mind.

Quarter Blessings

I meet people all the time.

At the bar I work at.

At the thrift store I work at.

Walking down the street.

Every place.

Very few of them have soul.

But some of the nicest people I ever meet

are the ones that hang out

at the liquor store by my house

bumming change.

They want nothing more than a quarter,

and when you give it to them

they say, "God Bless You."

And they mean it.

Then I watch the TV

and some preacher says that they need

Millions Of Dollars

to help them.

Help them what?

And if I sent them a quarter,

because they say send only what you can afford,

would they say, "God Bless You?"

I think not.

I believe those people at the liquor store

have more soul,

and I can afford their blessings.

I'm Sorry

We went to bed.

Once.

Well, almost went to bed.

As if on cue,

at the moment of penetration,

I cried.

I cried because you were not who I wanted

you to be.

Because it was too soon

after the end

of yet another torrid love affair,

and I felt so bad thinking of someone else.

So, I cried.

These things happen.

Waste It

I sit here and stare at my clock

for one full minute.

The only power I have over time

is to waste it.

If I try and find extra time

to spend with someone I love,

on those rare occasions

that I actually do love someone,

there aren't enough hours in a day.

But if I sit at home lonely

and watch the clock

for one full minute,

then two, then three…

The phone won't ring.

No knock at the door.

To truly waste time I must be lonely.

I must be alone.

Roommate Blues in the Key of E

My roommate tells me,

"You're a shitty guitar player."

"Hey man," I say, "I'm a songwriter!"

The guitar.

The bass.

The drums.

The words.

Put them all together

and it rocks.

Rock and Roll.

It's the song that counts.

Besides,

I don't think I'm that shitty

of a guitar player.

So I tell him,

"Yeah, well… you never hang up

your clothes.

You're a slob!"

And it just goes on

and on

from there.

Just a Thought

I wonder what it would be like

to wake up one day

and just know.

Know the bills were paid.

Know the rent was paid.

Know my car was in excellent running condition.

Know I could afford to buy groceries.

Know that my phone would never, ever,

be turned off again.

Know that I would never,

ever, have to pawn my guitar again.

There are people like that.

I wonder what they worry about.

Please God, Don't Let Me Go Crazy

My biggest fear

is a slow

but sure

decline

into insanity.

To end up

some babbling, unkempt

freak

pushing a shopping cart

down Santa Monica Blvd.

To be gawkcd at,

"I wonder what happened to her?"

When I wake up some mornings,

I have to fight myself for control

of myself.

I'm afraid I will open my mouth

and spew

angry and hostile words.

Verbal ugliness

in wide eyed terror,

mouth agape,

unable to stop.

To never find my way back.

Sometimes

I let it get close,

very close,

before shutting it off.

It's like a game.

Who will win?

Me, or the new crazy me?

Sometimes,

driving alone late at night

on the freeway,

I will close my eyes

and count to ten

for the hell of it.

Sometimes

I let myself believe

that I already am

slightly mad.

I think it's a valid fear.

Answer Me!

Seconds

Turn into minutes

Turn into hours

Turn into days

Turn into weeks

Turn into months

Turn into years

Turn into decades.

What the fuck

happened

to

my

life?

You In My Bed

You picked me up at the club.

You gave me a kiss.

You gave me a taste.

You gave me your number

and said, "This has only just begun."

You forgot your jacket at my place,

and 24 hours later

you're back at my house.

Back in my bed.

We're a tangle of sheets,

lipstick and sweat.

Nights like these, they feel like forever.

Since I got you in my bed,

I just can't get you out of my head.

It's Over

The telephone is ringing

right off the wall.

My head is screaming

"Shut up!"

They want to talk,

and I am running out of polite ways to say

I just don't give a shit.

There's always hell to pay

when someone wants to walk,

and someone wants to stay.

Sweating out confrontation,

I keep my distance,

marking time like miles.

Let's Call it Love

We're high wire lovers

doing dangerous dances.

We're empty threats

and parting glances.

We're subtle violence,

and hopeless romantics.

We ask too many questions,

and have all the answers.

You're an airtight alibi

when you walk thru the door.

Infidelity becomes you,

and I am never bored.

You do what you want.

I do as I please.

It keeps us on our toes.

it keeps us on our knees.

Slave

I'm a slave to my love life.

I've got to work hard

all of the time,

to satisfy you're curious needs.

I'm a slave to my vices,

and the games that we play.

I've got to work hard

all of the time,

to make sure you are never bored.

And I like it.

I'm a slave to my secrets,

my private hell.

I've got to work hard

all of the time.

Malicious thoughts

and unpopular wants

safely locked up inside my mind.

27

It seemed too soon

to be too late

with all of the answers

and none of the blame.

Venom in your words,

sugar in your tea,

a fortune in your lap,

offered no relief.

A tragic tale that's been over told,

another voice bought and sold.

Against all wishes.

Against all desire.

They made you a hero.

They made you a liar.

Warrior poet with a broken heart,

can't be mended.

Just torn apart.

8572 Santa Monica Blvd

I was the bartender.

You were the customer.

You said, "You make my eyes crazy."

I didn't charge you for your two Corona's

because you made me laugh out loud.

I could have said, "$6.50." But I didn't.

I could have said a lot of things,

but I didn't.

Because I knew I could get you in bed,

free beers or not.

I knew you would make me work for it.

That you wouldn't give it up

just like that.

I love the chase.

A Secular Day in Church

I like the way you smell.

The musky combination of frankincense

and cigarette smoke.

You smell like Catholicism.

I would like to fuck you in a Catholic church,

freeing you from any religious induced guilt

you may have.

I would suggest a few "Hail Mary's."

A few "Our Father's."

Then I would go down on you,

fucking you and kissing you

until you came.

Seemingly blasphemous,

but in fact the most sacred of acts

performed in the most sacred of places.

I am not a heathen.

On Sunday people perform the ritual

of getting dressed up and going to church.

They bring their Bible, their children,

their warped sense of right and wrong,

make a donation, go to confession,

and on Monday go about their lives.

In the end

they tally up all their Sundays spent in church,

and expect absolution.

I want to fuck you in a Catholic church

not to offend God,

but to spite them.

I would sit you down in one of those pews

and admire you in your Sunday best.

A lovely dress, perhaps from the 60's or 70's.

High heels, a garter belt, stockings, no panties,

and your hair down.

You know, the way I like you to dress.

You would spread your legs for me

so I could see you are already wet

at the thought of what we were about to do.

I would take my finger and remove a drop,

make the sign of the cross,

place it in my mouth,

then share it with a kiss.

I would kneel before you,

place my hands inside your thighs

and spread your legs,

saying a silent prayer of gratitude

before going down on you.

I would worship your pussy with my tongue,

desiring to serve only you.

I would welcome the sweet and familiar taste

of you in my mouth.

Your legs spread further apart

as my fingers tease your cunt.

You push yourself into me

until I slide inside.

We pick up a natural rhythm,

and you come quickly.

Silently.

Urgently.

I see a small patch of moisture

on the wooden bench.

It is beautiful and surreal.

It would be the closest thing

to a religious experience

I

have ever

had.

Sam

Just when I thought

I couldn't possibly love anymore…

Just when I thought

I couldn't feel anymore…

Just when I thought

I had finally found all the joy

life had to offer…

Just when I thought

I had everything

I could possibly want

to be happy and content…

Just when I thought I was complete…

My son was born.

We are Breeders

Are you scared?

Because I'm scared.

Sort of.

Not like,

"Oh my God! What have I done?"

or

"Oh my God! What am I going to do?"

Nothing like that.

It's crazy how far ahead

the mind wanders

with a child in the equation.

What switch was clicked?

I used to only think about

new music toys.

Now I think about Toys 'R' Us.

I even have a strong,

well informed opinion

on which is better:

Huggies or Pampers. (Huggies.)

I know that Playtex nipples suck,

and Even Flow rule.

But here is what is scary:

It's all fine.

Just like that,

these things mattered more

than the right guitar strings,

(GHS Boomers #10)

or writing a song

and working out the guitar and vocal parts.

Our whole world changed

in a matter of hours,

and we are fine.

Exhausted.

But otherwise,

just fine.

Been a Long Time Since I Rock and Rolled

I'm going on Tuesday

to play music

for the first time

in a long time.

How do I feel?

Somewhat excited.

Somewhat inconvenienced.

This is odd,

as I spent most of my life

eating/breathing/sleeping/

fucking/sucking/drinking/touching

all things Rock and Roll.

I lived for it.

I needed it,

and it needed me.

When I get there

I hope I feel it again.

But one thing is for sure,

I may stop playing music,

but I will never stop being a musician.

Quick Question

Is this the last love song

I'm ever gonna write?

Or just the last one while I'm poor?

Or just the last one tonight?

Post Prozac

It's Just Words

Writing is something

I have to do alone.

So that when I talk to myself,

or laugh out loud,

or cry in silence,

no one sees it,

no one hears it,

no one knows anything.

I write for myself.

If I wrote for others

I would stay shallow.

To write, to really write,

I have to dig down deep.

I have to risk looking like an asshole

to tell my truth.

A fool to share my thoughts.

A wimp to admit my feelings.

I have to be shameless

and insufferable

and not give a fuck.

And to write about love?

God damn, I simply have to

be able to cry at my own words.

To write strong

I have to be weak.

Alone.

Where no one can see me.

Idiot Me

I wasn't unlucky

in love.

Or out of love.

It really didn't matter,

because what I was

was lazy.

Too damn lazy

to care about myself,

let alone anyone else.

So if it looked right,

even if it felt wrong,

(Because sometimes all we've got to go on

is how we look getting there,

even when we are going nowhere in particular),

I'd do it.

I didn't have bad luck,

I was simply an idiot

making idiot choices.

My mouth said, "Yes,"

and everything else said, "No."

Make a wrong decision

and devote myself

to trying to make it right.

It gave me something to do.

I don't need to do that anymore.

It's What I Do

You know I am going to write about you.

Bleed all over the page.

Because I loved you fearlessly,

and you just couldn't.

You said you were brave.

You aren't.

Sorry.

I don't even know

how many broken hearts I have left in me.

And I don't know what makes me sadder,

the pain I am feeling

at this very moment,

or knowing I won't feel anything

after enough time goes by.

And these writings,

that are currently keeping

me sane and together?

They will become harmless pieces of paper,

in a pile with all the others

that have saved my life over the years.

And I won't ever really know why

you became so damn mean

and cold hearted.

Or even care.

After enough time has gone by.

three-sixteen-twelve

You asked me

if I'd ever seen a cat in heat.

So fucking random,

I knew you were the girl for me.

After several weeks,

we fell for each other. Hard.

We wanted to get married.

In Vegas.

By Elvis.

Hell, I never even wanted

to get married before.

Funny,

now that I think about it,

we never did decide

on old Elvis or young Elvis.

But I digress.

You came at me

with the very best of everything you had,

including an endearing story of a 15 year crush.

You wanted me,

and you did not back down or give up

until you had all of me.

My love.

My heart.

My devotion.

My trust.

My future

in your hands.

And once you did,

you had no idea what to do with me.

So you retreated

into insecurity,

misdirected anger,

projection,

and blah, blah, blah.

After a while

I couldn't take it anymore,

and told you as much.

Told you I wanted to talk about it.

To work thru it.

To work it out.

You told me,

"Just tell your friends

you dumped me because I'm a bitch

and I'm crazy."

Which is not entirely true.

I didn't dump her,

she dumped me.

Like it even matters.

Yellow

I've got more pills than problems,

but not enough to make me

forget how I feel,

so I leave them alone.

I am one tough and brave

motherfucker.

I take my pain quick.

And alone.

Maybe if I smoke enough cigarettes

I can get off this ride.

Heartache and hatred –

for the way you looked at me.

Anger and sadness –

for the things you said to me.

Drunk on disbelief –

that you threw it all away.

I am currently a cliché.

I am the baby in the bathwater.

and you?

You are a coward.

Late Last Night

After making myself

completely vulnerable.

Again.

By being completely honest.

Again.

Telling you I wanted nothing more

than for you to tell me,

to my face,

it was over.

Because in my arrogance,

or maybe because of

my trust in your words,

I refused to believe

you really wanted to let me go.

Or stopped loving me.

I promised you

I would never do you wrong.

Giving up without a fight seemed wrong.

So if someone rang the damn bell,

I didn't hear it.

Standing

You told me I was running,

when I was standing right there,

waiting for you to take it all back.

The name calling.

The cheap shot about my age.

Calling me a psycho

when I said I loved you

and wanted to work it out.

Well, now I am standing over here,

not waiting for you to take it all back.

It was never really mine, anyway,

so you can just keep it.

My side of the street is clean.

Hollywood Friends

I got a friend who says

being strung out is incredible.

The romantic junkie.

I got a friend who says

she lives for rock and roll.

But every time it gets close,

she falls apart.

I got a friend who says,

"True love is hard to find."

I have more friends like these

than any other kind.

April 13, 2010

Sitting in front of my shop.

Smoking a cigarette.

Mind wandering.

An image of you comes into focus.

I ask myself why?

Why does this girl keep showing up?

Maybe it's because she quoted

Bukowski to me

in an early and feverish exchange.

Maybe it's because she promised me

a slow dance,

and I told her something like,

"I would gladly charge hell

with a bucket of water in one hand,

and an Otis CD in the other,

just for the pure pleasure of holding you close

and feeling your breath against my neck."

And I meant it. Every word.

I have been a welcome voyeur,

checking in now and then.

Watching her lovers come and go

in a very public forum.

Anyone can watch, pay attention,

and learn.

"Too young," I say,

"to handle a woman like that."

"To naive," I say,

 "to understand the desires and needs

of a woman like that."

I would like to take her

out of her world for a minute.

Away from everyone she knows

and everywhere she feels safe,

and bring her into mine.

It's not much,

but we can laugh hard,

kiss hard,

fuck hard,

love hard,

ride hard,

play hard.

I can make a lasting impression on her mind

with my words and bad intentions.

On her pussy

with my lips and tongue and fingers and cock,

as I deliver on some of those bad intentions.

On her skin temporarily

with my mouth and teeth and finger tips

as they travel her body from neck to inner thigh

and linger in all the right places.

Then permanently, with my needles and ink.

At night we would sleep like lovers,

content and tangled up

in exhaustion and satisfaction.

And while she was asleep,

I would take that Bluebird out of her heart

and breathe life into him.

Tell him I love him, that he is beautiful,

then put him back before she woke up,

because she is too tough and clever for him

and she must never know

that he and I know differently.

Then I would send her back home,

knowing that we now owned

a little piece of each other.

Invisible

All those years I tried to sell my soul

to go unnoticed.

Except under the lights,

behind a shitty PA.

Don't hear me

unless I'm talking to you.

Don't see me

unless I'm singing to you.

Don't feel me

unless I'm touching you.

Don't notice me

let me slip on thru.

Thru my day.

Thru my night.

Thru my lovers.

Thru my life.

Now I'm pushing 50.

No one told me I'd just have to get old

to become invisible.

Up To Her Waist

"You think too much!"

Her words the color of agitation,

and she's right.

But along with all the annoying shit

I think about,

I think about my tongue in her mouth.

I think about my mouth on her neck.

I think about my fingers inside her.

I think about my hand on her ass.

I think about my body shoved up against hers.

I think about her voice in my ear.

She is ice cold.

My touch can't warm her.

My words can't soothe her.

My hands can't reach her.

If she let me in, she'd have to let herself out.

It's much safer in the shallow end.

Your Mouth

Tongue so sharp

cuts me to the bone.

Words so heavy

fall in me like a bomb.

Stuck in My Eye

Even at night,

when the glitter is rendered harmless,

I catch myself lost in thought.

How long have I been wandering

these long, empty hallways

this time?

Maybe, I think,

"If I knock lightly on enough doors,

she will answer."

Yeah, that is probably what I think.

Content to covet, though I am.

And that takes patience

with zero expectation.

Desire without context.

Honesty devoid of censorship.

And that takes courage.

Not the foolish kind, no,

but the kind that sets you free.

I will stop if you say "when."

I promise.

Until then,

I will look you right in the eye,

and you,

and only you,

will know my truth.

And Stay Away

That bitch heartache

took a seat right next to me.

I said, "Go away, fucker."

She swims in my pain

like an unwanted guest.

When I am at my worst,

she absolutely loves me.

She comes looking like

my best friend,

puts her arms around me

and holds me tight.

Whispers in my ear,

"It's me, baby."

ps. Fuck You

The honest truth is: I did nothing.

I ran my fingers down no other body.

I whispered in no other ear.

I kissed no other lips.

I shared no words of intimacy,

or lust or love with another.

Written or spoken.

But you just knew,

just knew I was lying and cheating.

The rage.

The accusations.

The ugly and malicious words

took us residence in my stomach.

A parasite feasting on verbs and nouns.

Twisting, burning, chewing me up.

I said, "You are wrong!"

You said, "You are a liar!"

How do I defend?

How do I fight something

that doesn't even exist?

I can't. I cannot.

So I did nothing

for months and months.

It was the only thing that kept me sane.

But she kept feeding that son of a bitch

that lived in my stomach

until it grew and grew

and consumed what little patience

and self respect

I had managed to hold onto.

I screamed

"Leave me the fuck alone!"

She didn't.

She hasn't.

She won't.

Found Words

While looking thru old notebooks

for lost words,

I found this:

"I think about you, too.

Live for you more.

Love only you, Cheri.

I am your whore."

Then two thoughts

immediately come to mind.

First off,

fuck you for getting strung out

and ruining everything we had.

Secondly,

what I wouldn't give for old school love,

with an old school girl,

who loves fearlessly,

following her heart.

Wrong Side of the Street

She walked into the place

like she owned it.

Ironic because,

I actually do.

And it made my heart beat

a little faster.

She has probably owned every room

she has ever entered

since God knows when.

A painted, fair skinned, high heeled

black cat of a beauty.

My temptation. My salvation.

Her departure? Just as memorable.

The slow good-bye,

one arm casually, innocently

wrapped around my waist.

Mine: Same. Not so innocent.

Enjoying the feel of her body

pressed up against mine.

Reminding myself not to flirt,

because I know what side of the line I live on.

So I keep my hands,

my mouth,

my words,

where they are supposed to be.

Not a problem.

But my thoughts…

well,

they go where ever

they damn well please.

The Long Ride

I am bored with vapid beauty.

Exhausted by toxic beauty.

Uninspired by women too young

to be considered anything but girls, really.

I want. I desire. I crave.

A woman.

I dream of a bad ass femme

with a wicked sense of humor,

a closet full of high heels

and black leather boots,

to take that long ride.

Arms wrapped around me.

Legs pressed against mine.

Holding on tight because she wants to,

not because she has to.

It's loud, we'd have to shout to be heard,

so instead we lean into the curves

and roll with the straight-aways.

Words will come later.

In the quiet, dark places.

Nothing before matters.

Nothing after is of consequence.

Just right fucking here.

Right fucking now.

I will meet her one day,

and it will be simply beautiful

I've Got a Pill For That

I take six pills a day.

I take pills for the pills

that get in the way

of my six pills a day.

I take pills for my thoughts.

I take pills for my brain.

I take pills for my fears.

I take pills for my pain.

Sometimes seven.

Sometimes ten.

It all depends

on the shape I'm in.

The Sound of You

Sitting in my back office

at the tattoo shop,

I hear the

click – click – click

of high heels on the tile floor,

and my heart skips a beat.

I look up, expecting to see her.

So beautiful,

she still takes my breath away.

Then my heart sinks as I realize

she is no longer.

That she only existed

for brief and rare moments.

So rare, in fact, I can probably

count them on two hands

over 5 years.

But those moments were sublime.

Sexy. Passionate. Compassionate.

Tender. Loving. Understanding.

Patient. Sweet. Funny.

Then they would disappear,

just as quickly as they arrived.

Gone.

I could not sustain them

no matter how hard I tried.

And believe me, I tried.

Regardless,

once in a while,

when I hear the

click – click – click

of high heels on tile,

I will smile.

We did have some good times.

NYC

It's like a bad dream,

we're moving slow and helpless.

We're not flying over rooftops.

We're not innocent and shapeless.

We're not looking for answers,

or making up excuses.

We're just holding on tight,

and trying not to lose us.

Junkies

I learned a lot about junkies

while living in Hollywood.

For example, I learned how to tell

which of your friends are junkies.

They are the ones who call you.

Three times a month.

To borrow $25.

To pay their phone bill.

Like the Others

Eventually,

they all do it.

Give me shit.

Give me shit

for being a writer.

Give me shit

for being me.

Charming at first, I imagine.

Fun, wordy flirtations and

hand written love letters.

Then, without fail,

comes the obvious disappointment.

That I want to be home.

That I want to be alone

with my notebooks

and my pencils.

Because writers

write.

No choice, really.

Either that or complete misery.

And angry girlfriends, like you,

mock me.

And become angry ex girlfriends.

Beware of Lemurs

I am all words.

You are the silence that encourages them.

I am all truth.

Your are the silent liar.

I am fearless.

You are the quiet coward.

You gave me a written warning,

disguised as a love letter.

Three pages.

Front and back.

Retrospect, baby,

is a bitch.

You are a passive/aggressive

mind fuck

feigning communication.

Good luck with that.

The Last Word

I have a blank piece of paper

and a Mirado Black Warrior #2 pencil.

I have the desire to write.

Something. Anything.

Blank paper taunts me.

Dares me.

If I walk away, it wins.

I recall my muse of thirteen years.

She left me five years ago

for crystal meth, Coors light

and my good friend, Christa

Fucked in the ass by the three C's.

Those were some dark days,

but I don't want to write about that.

I don't want to write about the hurt.

The heartache.

The disbelief,

Or the fact that they ultimately

had more in common than we did:

The drugs and the drink.

I sure as hell don't want to write

about a cut so deep

it left me drowning in my own blood

for years.

Don't even want to think about that

ever again.

But fuck you, paper

this time I win.

Lyrics

Give Me

If I had a dollar
for every fucking thing
I should have been paid for,
I'd be living like a queen.

But dedication means nothing.
Devotion doesn't count.
Passion is over looked.
Even in large amounts.

Give it. Give it, to me.
Give it all. Give it all to me.

I should have my way,
'cuz I know what's best
I should be rich. I should be famous.
Aloof and unimpressed.

But I got one hand reaching out.
One foot in the grave.
I'm waving bye-bye.
I'm reaching to be saved.

Give it, give it to me.
Give it all, give it all to me.

Punk Rock Girl

Punk Rock Girl says,
"Can't you play a little faster?
I only like the music
when it goes real fast."
Punk Rock Girl says,
"Can't you play a little louder?
Just a little louder,
'cuz I like it like that."

Punk Rock Girl says,
"Can't you play a little faster?
Can't you play a little louder,
man, can't you do that?"
Punk Rock Girl,
she don't wanna hear no slow songs.
She don't see the point
in crap like that.

Punk Rock Girl says,
"Can't you play a little faster?
Can't you play a little louder,
man, can't you do that?"

Punk Rock Girl says,
"The music doesn't move me,
it only kicks my ass
when it goes real fast."

137

Pretty, Pretty

Hey there pretty pretty,
tell me what you gonna do?
Got your finger on the trigger
when no ones watching you.
Good times, bad times,
they all feel the same,
when you're looking at
looking at, looking at insane.

Hey there pretty pretty,
tell me what you gonna do?
Making so much noise,
now all eyes are on you.
You got pretty girls and pretty boys,
hearts full of tragedy.
Now you're looking at, looking at,
looking at me.

Hey pretty pretty – you think
the drugs look good on you.
Hey pretty pretty – you got
Hollywood eyes and a jacked up tattoo.
You got Rock and Roll dreams.
You want to fuck a Rock and Roll star.
Hey pretty pretty - at your best
you're just a gorgeous mess
that's gone too far.

Hey there, pretty pretty,
What do you think of me now?
Still got pinned eyes for me,
or did I bring you down somehow?

Hey pretty pretty - you think
the drugs look good on you.
Hey pretty pretty - you got
Hollywood eyes and a jacked up tattoo.
You got Rock and Roll dreams.
You want to fuck a Rock and Roll star.
Hey pretty pretty - at your best
you're just a gorgeous mess
that's gone too far.
Hey pretty, pretty...

Trip

Guilt trip, crack the whip.
Talk so slick you
know I just might slip.
Love trip, another miss.
The slip of a tongue
makes for a desperate kiss.

I just want to go to sleep,
but I am too God Damn tired.
I just want to tell the truth,
but I am a God Damn liar.

God trip, contradiction.
The road to hell is paved
with false conviction.
Mind trip, set me free.
My fear is failure
and slow insanity

I just want to go to sleep,
but I am too God Damn tired.
I just want to tell the truth,
but I am a God Damn liar.

Hard Times

I don't want to talk about it,
keep it buried deep inside.
Living with it all these years.
A special place for special lies.
Looking tough but feeling lonely,
lock the door, I take a fall.
Think those thoughts that drive me crazy.
No one answers when I call

I know you just want to spare me the grief
of life's little horrors, but I feel like a thief
for the pleasures stolen.
Hard times come cheap.

I love the way you let me down,
hard and fast I'm on the ground.
No regrets that I can see.
Wrapped up in endless apologies
So, what you gonna do, hurt me?
Someone did that years ago.
I fight to live a life of truth,
while I get thrown too and fro.

I know you just want to spare me the grief
of life's little horrors, but I feel like a thief
for the pleasures stolen.
Hard times come cheap.

Every 6 Minutes

Every six minutes, someone says no.
And every six minutes,
she gets ignored.
It's not what you're wearing.
It's not where you've been.
The fact that they think so
tells you something about sin.

Every six minutes, a woman cries.
Because every six minutes,
her pleas are denied.
No one's asking for it.
It's no woman's secret desire.
The fact that they think so
is a man made lie.

The passing of time,
 brings you closer to me.
The cycle of injustice,
 keeps you free.
I've got .38 special
reasons at my side.
Face the ultimate "no" big boy,
This time I'll decide.

If I had a bullet,
every six minutes

I'd know just where to put it,
every six minutes.
One in your heart,
might be a good start.
And one in your brain,
just might ease my pain.

The passing of time,
brings you closer to me.
The cycle of injustice,
keeps you free.
I've got .38 special
reasons at my side.
Face the ultimate "no" big boy.
This time I'll decide.
If I had a bullet,
every six minutes.
I'd know just where to put it,
every six minutes.

The Ugly

Bring on the ugly.
Bring on the shit.
You bring me something,
I just can't fix.
I'll make you ugly,
might do the trick.
No one can fix you.
You make me sick.

You bring out the worst in me.
And you bring out the hate in me.
My wrath is something you can see.
Now you're ugly.

Can't see you coming,
but we feel you leave.
Don't see you're own messes,
and you don't feel the grief.
When you bring on the ugly.
When you bring on the shit.
You bring me something,
I just can't fix.

You bring out the worst in me.
And you bring out the hate in me.
My wrath is something you can see.
Now you're ugly.

Did I take revenge on my broken brother?
Shall I make amends, should I even bother?
Did he pay the price for so many others?
Because I don't feel a thing
for that sick mother fucker.

You bring out the worst in me.
And you bring out the hate in me.
My wrath is something you can see.
Now you're ugly.

Bitter Pill

They say it's lonely at the top.
Let me tell ya, man,
it kills at the bottom.
Where you have to be remembered first,
Before you can be forgotten.

One plus one plus one makes three.
Me and you and you and me.
What's the price, how much is free?
When one and one
and one makes me.

They say it's lonely at the top.
Let me tell ya, man,
it kills at the bottom.

4 into 3

And now we're cleaning up the messes.
And filling in the spaces.
And picking up the pieces
of the choices that break us
from four into three.

Jagged ends and sharp edges.
We'll wear each other down
in all the right places.
And we can face this.
These are the choices that make us.

It's like a bad dream,
we're moving slow and helpless.
We're not flying over rooftops,
we're not innocent and we're not shapeless.
We're not looking for answers,
or making up excuses.
We're just holding on tight,
and trying not to lose us.

And now we're cleaning up the messes.
And filling in the spaces.
And picking up the pieces
of the choices that breaks us
from four into three.

Jagged ends and sharp edges.
We'll wear each other down
in all the right places.
And we can face this.
These are the choices that make us.
These are the choices that take us.
These are the choices that break us.
These are the choices that make us.
Stay…

Hey, Jesus

I woke up on the wrong side of the bed
again today.
I spent half the morning smoking cigarettes,
just like yesterday.
I wonder what I'm doing
over coffee that's cold and say,
"Time flies, but no, not me.
Thank God the rent is paid."

Hey Jesus, I know you're up there,
'cuz I talk to you each day.
I agonize over everything
while I hope you keep me safe.
Hey Jesus... from the psychos.
Hey Jesus... from the freaks.
Hey Jesus... from the bad guys.
But please, oh please, oh please....
keep me safe from me.

I really do know better than to indulge
myself this way.
So now I'm stuck with no direction,
just like yesterday.
I got no place to breathe,
from room to room I roam.
Sleeping bodies litter the furniture,
inside my happy home.

Hey Jesus I know you're up there,
'cuz I talk to you each day.
I agonize over everything
while I hope you keep me safe.
Hey Jesus... from the psychos.
Hey Jesus... from the freaks.
Hey Jesus... from the bad guys.
But please, oh please, oh please...
keep me safe from me.

That Was Me

Have you ever been just a little bit crazy?
Have you ever gone just a little bit mad?
When the voices in you head,
they can't be yours,
but they're the only ones you have.
They stay like an unwanted guest.
They won't give you no rest.

Got no use for lovers,
got no use for my friends.
I lock myself up 'cuz in the dark
I see the best.
I'm completely alone,
I'm completely unfree.
And my only thought is,
"Yeah, the world owes me!"

Ever felt a pain so deep
you just can't touch it?
Ever looked in the mirror
and wondered where you went?
Ever walked away with no apologies?

'Till nothing seemed to work
and nothing seemed to fit?
'Cuz that was me. It was me.

Have you ever gone
slightly crazy?
Have you ever been
just a little bit mad?

My Favorite Sin

6141 Afton Place was my home.
Junkies, thieves, red necks and queens.
Rock and roll stars, and freaks like me.

I try and leave this place
where the sidewalk screams.
And the court yard's littered
with broken dreams.
But those dirty, dirty angels
keep pulling me in.
Promising me more of my favorite sin.

35 flew by near Sunset and Vine.
I'm not getting any younger.
Hollywood is killing me,
this towns a mother fucker.

I try and leave this place
where the sidewalk screams.
And the court yard's littered
with broken dreams.
But those dirty, dirty angels
keep pulling me in.
Promising me more of my favorite sin.

My heart is wrung out.
My friends are strung out.

Lies must be told,
and veins must be fed.
I'm walking thru this town
with the walking dead.

I try and leave this place
where the sidewalk screams.
And the court yard's littered
with broken dreams.
But those dirty little angels
keep pulling me in.
Promising me more of my favorite sin.

Dead in your Head

You want to kill me inside your head,
then you can pretend that I'm really dead.
Your poetry's in motion, upside down.
I'm dripping off your walls
without a sound.
Little ghosts inside your head.
Little angels filled with dread.
Light a candle and go to sleep.
Tomorrow's pain is just as cheap.
You're walking thru my mind.
You're swimming in my veins.
Thoughts of you make me insane.

You're lips are moving, words that cut.
But when I kiss you, you shut up.
Little ghosts inside your head.
Little angels filled with dread.
Light a candle and go to sleep.
Tomorrow's pain is just as cheap.
You want to kill me inside your head,
then you can pretend that I'm really dead.

Ms. Tweak

She says, "Bad luck follows me around.
All my friends have let me down.
I don't need this dress, these drugs, this town,
these people, this party,
yeah, it's bringing me down."

She says, "I never used to live like this,
I had it all and walked away from it.
I don't need these problems,
this drama, this shit.
It's 3am, and I'm losing my grip."

With a mouth full of lies,
and a heart full of sighs,
"Why me, or Lord, why me?" she cries.
"Cuz everyone else is so fucked up.
And everything else is so fucked up.
And it always finds me, it's just my luck."

Ms. Tweak lives in Hollywood.
Looking up at hell,
she thinks she's got it so good.
She don't need no family, no friends, no man.
She don't need nothing,
man, she don't give a damn.

With a mouth full of lies,

and a heart full of sighs,
"Why me, oh Lord, why me?" she cries
"Cuz everyone else is so fucked up.
And everything else is so fucked up.
And it always finds me, it's just my luck."

She says, "Blah, blah, blah…"
She says nothing at all.

Narcotic Buddies

Narcotic buddies,
my Hollywood friends.
You're a stomachache,
twist and bend.
You say nothing
I haven't heard before.
You got nothing,
and you want some more.

My narcotic buddies
are wearing me out.
With your tragic tales
and your hand always out.
My narcotic buddies,
always want my money.
My narcotic buddies
are full of shit and honey.

Here's to all my friends
who sold me out to stay well.
My narcotic buddies,
I bid you farewell.
The road less traveled
takes you away.
Break and decay,
burn and erase.

My narcotic buddies
are wearing me out.
With your tragic tales
and your hand always out.
My narcotic buddies
always want my money.
My narcotic buddies
are full of shit and honey.

Down

I said shit, baby, baby,
now what is this?
You're pissed and you're telling me,
"It's like that, it's like this."
Well let me tell you something,
man, just give it a rest.

I'm going down, down.
I'm going down.
I said down, baby down.
You're bringing me down.

I'm not big on the little things
that mean so much.
Like an endearing look,
or a strategic touch.
But if you'd just leave me alone
I could do so much.

I'm going down, down.
I'm going down.
I said down, baby down.
You're bringing me down.

And I don't want to talk,
'cuz it don't matter.
I don't want to know,

'cuz it don't matter.
And I don't give a shit,
'cuz it don't matter.

I got you on the telephone,
you won't give me a break.
It seems like everybody wants
a piece of my cake.
But for a girl who wants it all,
I get nothing but shake.

I'm going down, down.
I'm going down.
I said down, baby down
You're bringing me down.

And I don't want to talk,
'cuz it don't matter.
I don't want to know,
'cuz it don't matter.
And I don't give a fuck,
'cuz it don't matter.

Sometimes I get so bitter,
it makes me feel better.

Painting Jesus

Got Jesus in my garage,
and he's getting cold.
Feeling to neglected to
save my soul.
Gonna bring him in,
gonna set him by the fire.
Promised him more,
now I'm feeling like a liar.

Painting Jesus is my solution.
Been so lazy,
now I'm seeking absolution.
Painting Jesus red and gold.
Painting Jesus beautiful
to save my soul.

I think he understands
and can appreciate,
good things can come to those
who are habitually late.
Don't go to church on Sunday,
don't get down on my knees.
Jesus sits on my porch,
and we're both quite pleased.

Painting Jesus is my solution.
Been so lazy,
now I'm seeking absolution.
Painting Jesus red and gold.
Painting Jesus beautiful
to save my soul.
Save my soul.
Gonna save my soul.

Too Many Shannon's

Blondes from hell
calling me on the phone.
For a good time drive
to the comforts of home.
Ten hours in a truck, it gets better still.
We were kept awake against our will.
And now tomorrow is today.
We didn't get to sleep,
and now were gonna play.

Blondes from hell,
those girls on the go.
Blondes from hell,
they want to rock and roll.
"Too many Shannon's"
is written on the lift.
Back to the bomb shelter,
the ride is worth the risk.

Lots of Jolt cola,
too many cigarettes.
The new mailboxes arrive,
it don't get better than this.
Many fond memories
to carry with us always.
Peroxide, speed,
and bathroom lines

into the hallway.

Blondes from hell,
those girls on the go.
Blondes from hell,
they want to rock and roll.
"Too many Shannon's"
is written on the lift.
Back to the bomb shelter,
the ride is worth the risk.

Some of those girls are my best friends.
Corpse Grinders rule to the bitter end.

My New Gun

You got to fight the world to save it,
it's out of control.
You got to fight men
with bullets for logic.
You got to fight men
with guns for soul.
I bought a gun today.
Now's the time
for a revolution of my mind.
I bought a gun today,
can't you see?
We need a revolution
of the sensibilities.

My neighborhood is,
my neighborhood is,
my neighborhood is,
filled with crime.
Guy at my window,
looking in my window.
Guy at my window,
beat him blind.
My neighborhood is,
my neighborhood is,
my neighborhood is
in rapid decline.
I bought a gun today.

Always a Bridesmaid, Never a Bride

All my life is an in between,
waiting to say what I really mean.
On the verge of some big thing,
just out of touch and just out of reach.
I'm on the outside looking in.
I'm waiting for the wait to end.

I close my mouth and shut my eyes,
to all the things that I despise.
I close my mouth and shut my eyes,
I'm always a bridesmaid, never a bride.

It runs right thru me to my very soul.
Keeps it all together and I can't let go.
My only grip, it's my only hope.
You've got a hold of that string,
you gotta let me go.
You hate your fears, or so it seems.
You taunt my life and you mock my dreams.

I close my mouth and shut my eyes,
to all the things that I despise.
I close my mouth and shut my eyes,
I'm always a bridesmaid, never a bride.

Hey! That's Mine.

There is no alter in my home.
I burn white candles when I'm alone.
I draw black hearts because
it pleases me.
Self indulgence has set me free.

That belongs to me. Hey, that's mine.
I love you baby, but I haven't got the time.
Because all I ever think about
is me myself and I.

My day starts promptly at 3pm,
when I move six feet
to my desk from the bed.
Without a word, let the ritual begin.
Coffee, cigarettes, some paper and a pen.

I keep your picture on my desk.
I keep my feelings to myself.
Some things I might fail to mention,
I keep up on the shelf
with my good intentions.

That belongs to me. Hey, that's mine.
I love you baby, but I haven't got the time.
Because all I ever think about
is me, myself and I.

No Way Out

Tension. Can you feel it?
The monster in my head, they come to life.
They whisper in my ear.
What do they say?
No one, no one gets out of here alive.

There's now way out…

Waking up can be such a chore.
Daily life can be such a bore.
Well, I do it every day,
and I wonder, wonder
what the hell for?
Killing time and knocking on,
knocking on locked doors.

There's no way out…
I keep looking, but there's no way out.
And I keep trying, but there's no way out.

Little Brother

The bible says we gotta reap what we sow,
but someone else tended our garden
so many years ago.
Plant this seed and watch it grow.
Hey little brother, how were we to know?
That the seeds of shame
grow in the shadow of doubt,
and feed the silence you can't live without.
Hey little brother, how were we to know?
The lines were drawn wrong a long time ago.
And we don't have to talk about it.

Kind words for you, with this I console.
We took our punishment well
so many years ago.
Move us away and watch us grow.
Hey little brother, how were they to know?
That the seeds of shame
grow in the shadow of doubt,
and feed the silence you can't live without.
I said hey, little brother,
how were we to know?
The lines were drawn wrong
a long time ago.
And we don't have to talk about it.

Sweet Pea Blues

Our first date was 22 hours long.
And our first kiss was the sweetest
I'd ever known.
You smell like cigarettes.
You smell like frankincense.
You taste like a catholic.
You sounded like an optimist.
What else could I do? I fell for you.

I know I put you in
a perpetual spin.
And I'm sorry about that letter I wrote,
but that shit, it had to end.
But it's not over 'till it's over.
I can't be everything,
but I can sure be your lover.
So take your time
and think it over.

I spun a web of hope
right around my heart.
And I wore it on my sleeve
right from the very start.
You say, "Hesitate and masturbate,"
of potential lovers who made you wait.

Well, now it's up to you.
It's time to make a move.
I say baby, baby, baby, baby
lose those brain spin blues.
Because baby, baby, baby, baby
now it's time to say fuck you.

Some People

We're five cheap numbers from LA.
We look good and we can play.
We may smoke, and we may drink,
but we live clean and we want peace.
Peace on earth. Piece of mind.
A piece if ass and a piece of the pie.

Some people don't like us
'cuz were girls in a band.
Some people shake their heads
and don't understand.
Some people want to know,
"Are you a girl or a boy?"
Some people must be bored
if that brings them joy.
Some people.

When the going gets tough, we don't run.
When the going gets tough, we have fun.
"Cuz life's too short not to be pleased.
We don't ask much, just give us these:
Peace on earth. Piece of mind.
A piece of ass and a piece of the pie.

Good To Be Bad

Tattooed and tattered,
you wear black well.
You walk the room baby, I can tell.
It feels so good to be bad.
It feels so good to be bad.

Come on baby, don't shy away.
There's lots of fun in danger
when there's hell to pay.
Come on baby, don't you hesitate.
Come on baby, don't you make me wait.
I've been waiting for you.

You can come a little closer.
You can fill up my head.
With the time of day,
and where the money's spent.
But you and I know
it's desire that thrills.
You and I know
it's desire that thrills.

Park it up the street,
let's keep out of sight.
It's the feel of you,
the sound of the night.

It feels so good to be bad.
It feels so good to be bad.

Come on baby, I just want a touch.
If I can lose it all is a touch,
a touch too much?
Come on baby, don't you hesitate.
Come on baby, don't you make me wait.
I've been waiting for you.
Yeah you.

You can come a little closer.
You can fill up my head.
with the time of day,
and all those things that you said.
But you and I know
it's desire that thrills.
You and I know
it's desire that thrills.

Where Are You?

Where are you?
I call you up, but you're not home.
You better not be late,
and you better be alone.
I want to chat you up,
but you're not there.
Do you know I'm calling?
Do you really care?

Where are you?
You're supposed to be at home.
Where are you?
And why aren't you
picking up your telephone?
Where are you?
You know I hate that machine.
When I don't know where you are,
nothing is the same.

I call you up, but you're not there.
Better get home soon,
or I lose my mind, I swear.
I want to say "I love you."
And that you're missed.
But no one answers,
and I'm getting really pissed.
Where are you?

Bigger, Better, Faster, More

I'm looking for a boy.
I'm looking for a girl.
Unspecified, open mind.
Sounds like a lie, like a waste of my time.

I should know better than that.
So much better than that
I want bigger, better, faster, more.

I bend over backwards baby,
to satisfy you.
Your wish is my command.
You believe that?
Well, shame on you.

You should know better than that.
So much better than that.

I want bigger, better, faster, more.

Just throw him in the car, he'll be fine.
Because the very next day
he won't remember a thing.
Because when Danny takes a drink,
he can't stop at one.

Drink and think.
Drink at school.
Drink and drive.
Drink and party.
Danny takes a drink just to survive.

Drink, drink, drink, drink, drink.

Post Nuclear Celebration Party Song

No more phone calls, no one's home
Where are my friends, am I alone?
Is this now anarchy, is this real?
The bombs have all fallen
against my will.

It's a beautiful planet.
It's a wonderful life.
A post nuclear celebration,
an after the bomb bash.
I'm having a party all by myself.
I've invited the world,
but everyone's dead.
Shall I comb my hair?
Shall I wait on guests?
It's getting late, I'll just wait on death.

Now I drink from a radioactive cup.
Where's my God, did he fuck up?
No one thought we'd see this day,
when we'd all die in the same way.
No rich or poor. Right or left.
Black and white died the same death.

A post nuclear celebration,
an after the bomb bash.
I'm having a party all by myself.

I've invited the world,
but everyone's dead.
Shall I comb my hair?
Shall I wait on guests?
It's getting late, I'll just wait on death.

It's a beautiful planet, at least what's left.
It's a wonderful life, except for the death.

Sam

Six days in a wire nest,
tangled up in what's best.
I reach in and I touch his hand.
I take a seat and I make a stand.

I'm gonna watch him like a TV.
Blue eyes to melt me.
Feel him like a freight train,
nothing's going to be the same.

I get no sleep, I guess I don't need it.
When the hunger comes we got to feed it.
Around the clock, seven days a week
I can't think and I don't sleep.

He holds my world
in the palm of his hand.
My fate is sealed.
They don't, but the should give a damn.

I'm gonna watch him like a TV.
Blue eyes to melt me.
Feel him like a freight train,
nothing's going to be the same.

I get no sleep, I guess I don't need it.
When the hunger comes we got to feed it.
Around the clock, seven days a week.
I can't think and I don't sleep.

Ugly World

There's a part of us that turns to see
the suffering all around and says,
"Better you than me."
It's easy enough when it's on TV.
Across the road or in the house
down the street.
"Well, if I were them, if they were me…"
So easy to judge, so hard to be free.

Why is it such an ugly world?
How can love end in death at 5am
in the hall on the floor?
Why is it such an ugly world?
In the eyes of that child,
no one listening,
no one helped,
no one heard.
Why is it such an ugly world?

What you going to do
when the world goes crazy?
What you going to do
when you're all alone?
Can you tell that kid
his life's worth living?
Thank God he'll never ask me.

We can call the police
from behind our locked doors.
And open when it's safe
and view the horror.
Then we get a closer look,
whether we want it or not.
We can cry for strangers,
and everything that's wrong.

There's a part of us that turns to see
the suffering all around and says,
"Better you than me."

Why is it such an ugly world?

Hollywood

Girls on Sunset, you pay the price.
Young boys on Santa Monica.
Everybody's got a vice.
Where LAPD run wild in the street.
Abusing their authority,
opposing you and me.
Obey all traffic laws, that's my advice.
Or get a night stick up your ass
Ain't this the life?
In Hollywood…

I know a lot of actors.
I know a lot of stars.
Hiding behind their drinks
at the local gay bars.
Where money keeps you safe,
buy silence from the press.
Mini cams, reporters,
like vultures get the rest.
See the punks trash clubs
on the news at four.
Edit out the riot squad
onto cutting room floor.
In Hollywood…

Prey for Rock & Roll

My life is three chords,
so let me finish.
Waited too damn long
for my 15 minutes.
Got a skinhead on my couch.
Ex junkie's in my bed.
Roadies passed out on the floor,
the fun, it never ends.

It's true, it's true,
I'm poor but I'm happy.
It's true, it's true,
I'm broke but I'm fine.
It's true, it's true,
I'm poor but I'm happy.
It's true, it's true,
'cuz all this nothin' is mine.

Love don't last, won't dig that hole.
They all complain,
I'm prey for rock and roll.
No record deal, won't sell my soul.
They all complain,
I'm prey for rock and roll.

Nothing used to matter
except half past three.
And the sweet, sweet taste
of infidelity.
Forget about what's right,
when being wrong is much more fun.
Down and out in Hollywood,
that's how the game is won.

It's true, it's true,
there's a whore living in my heart.
It's true, it's true,
yeah, yeah, yeah, yeah.
It's true, it's true,
there's a whore living in my heart.
It's true, it's true,
she was bad, bad, bad.
Love don't last, won't dig that hole.
They all complain,
I'm prey for rock and roll.
No record deal, won't sell my soul.
They all complain,
I'm prey for rock and roll.

Acknowledgements:

Cover Photo by Morgan Anderson.

Pre Prozac Photo by Carol McElligott.

Post Prozac Photo by Cheri Lovedog.

Lyrics Photo by FatChance Productions, NYC.

Back Photo by Jewels Youhas.

Lady Justice Art by Zack Gaylord.

For More Information on Cheri Lovedog Please Visit

www.writelouder.com

CHERI LOVEDOG

Printed in Dunstable, United Kingdom

68235338R00107